MAY -- 2014

CHICAGO
Cubs

BY K. C. KELLEY

Published by The Child's World®
1980 Lookout Drive • Mankato, MN 56003-1705
800-599-READ • www.childsworld.com

Acknowledgments
The Child's World®: Mary Berendes, Publishing Director
Red Line Editorial: Editorial direction
The Design Lab: Design
Amnet: Production
Design Elements: Photodisc

Photographs ©: Gene J. Puskar/AP Images, cover, 1, 2; Zuma
Press/Icon SMI, 5; Warren Wimmer/CSR/Icon SMI, 6, 25
(center), 26, 27; AP Images, 9, 22 (inset); Scott Kane/Icon SMI,
10; Shutterstock Images, 13; Design Lab, 14; Nam Y. Huh/AP
Images, 17; Amy Sancetta/AP Images, 18; M. Spencer Green/
AP Images, 21; John Cordes/Icon SMI, 22; Juan Salas/Icon
SMI, 25 (top); Alison Henley/Shutterstock Images, 25 (bottom)

ISBN 9781623239756
LCCN 2013947262

Printed in the United States of America
Mankato, MN
December, 2013
PA02188

ABOUT THE AUTHOR

K. C. Kelley has written dozens of books on baseball and other sports for young readers. He has also been a youth baseball coach and called baseball games on the radio. His favorite team is the Boston Red Sox.

Cover: Starlin Castro, Shortstop

C O N T E N T S

Go, Cubs!

The Cubs have been in Chicago for more than 100 years. That's how long it has been since the team won a **World Series**. Ouch! However, their fans remain **loyal** and loud. The "Cubbies" are among baseball's best-loved teams. Let's meet the Cubs!

Luis Valbuena (right) congratulates Carlos Villanueva after Villanueva scored a run at Wrigley Field.

Who Are the Cubs?

The Chicago Cubs are a team in baseball's National League (NL). The NL joins with the American League (AL) to form Major League Baseball. The Cubs play in the Central Division of the NL. The division winners and two wild-card teams get to play in the league playoffs. The playoff winners from the two leagues face off in the World Series. The Cubs have won two World Series championships.

Travis Wood throws a pitch in a game against the Los Angeles Dodgers.

Where They Came From

The Chicago Cubs haven't always been the Cubs. The NL had its first season in 1876. The Chicago White Stockings played in that first NL season. They became the Colts in 1890, then the Orphans in 1898. Finally, in 1903, they got their current name. The Cubs have always played in Chicago. They have been in their current ballpark longer than any other NL team.

The 1929 Cubs team played at Wrigley Field,
just like the present-day team.

9

Who They Play

The Chicago Cubs play 162 games each season. That includes about 19 games against each of the other teams in their division. The Cubs have won three NL Central championships. The other NL Central teams are the Cincinnati Reds, the Milwaukee Brewers, the Pittsburgh Pirates, and the St. Louis Cardinals. The Cubs and the Cardinals are big **rivals**. Their games always get the fans charged up! The Cubs also play some teams from the AL. Their AL **opponents** change every year.

Darwin Barney turns a double play against the St. Louis Cardinals.

Where They Play

Wrigley Field has been the home of the Cubs since 1914. It is the oldest ballpark in the NL. Many of the walls are made of brick. The **outfield** fence is covered with bright green ivy plants! Some buildings are very close to Wrigley Field. Fans can sit on their roofs to watch the game! The area around the beloved ballpark is fun on game days. It's called "Wrigleyville." The ballpark was the last in the majors to get lights for night baseball. Until 1988, all Cubs home games were day games!

This famous sign hangs over the main entrance to Wrigley Field.

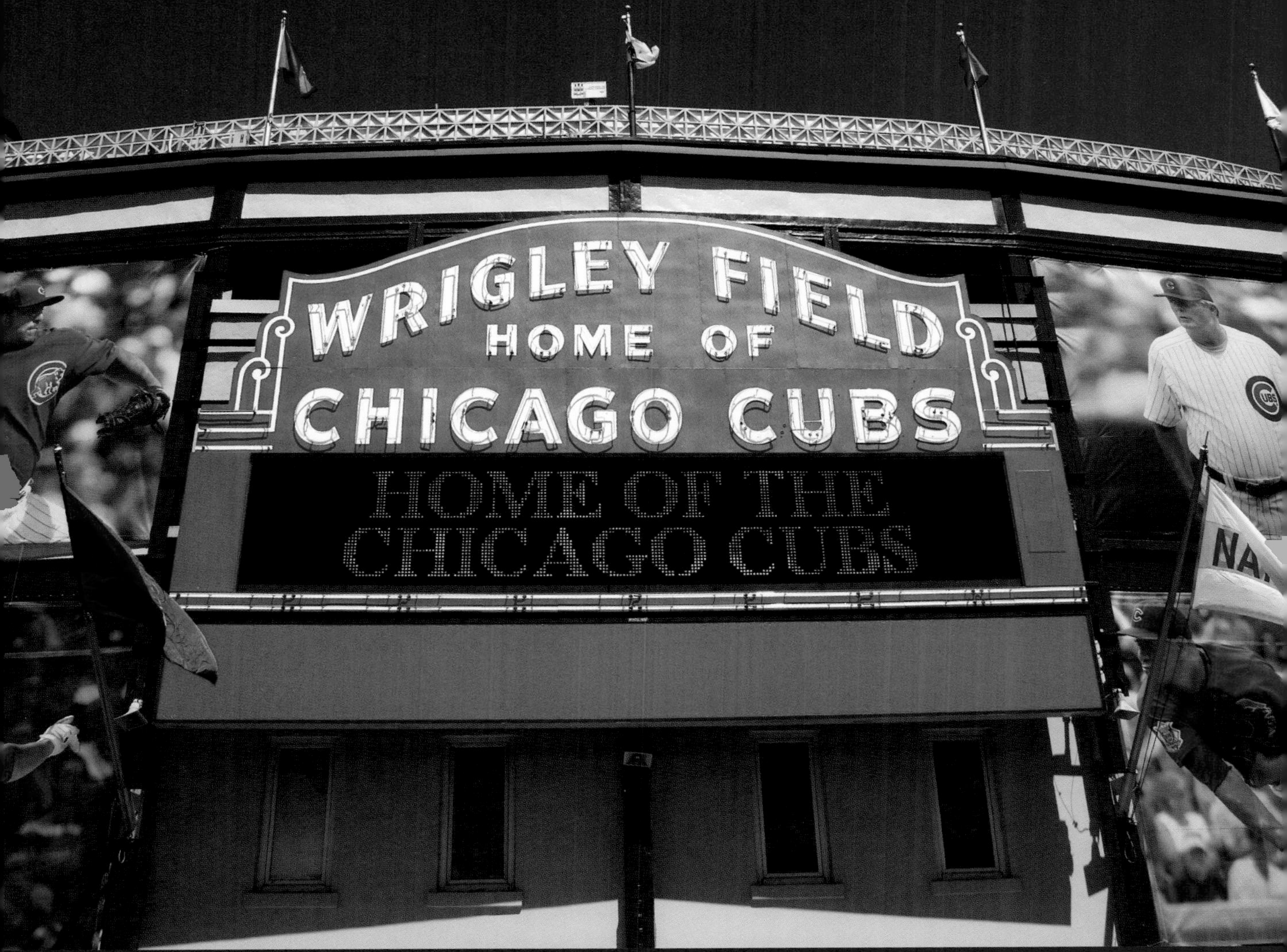
WRIGLEY FIELD
HOME OF
CHICAGO CUBS
HOME OF THE
CHICAGO CUBS

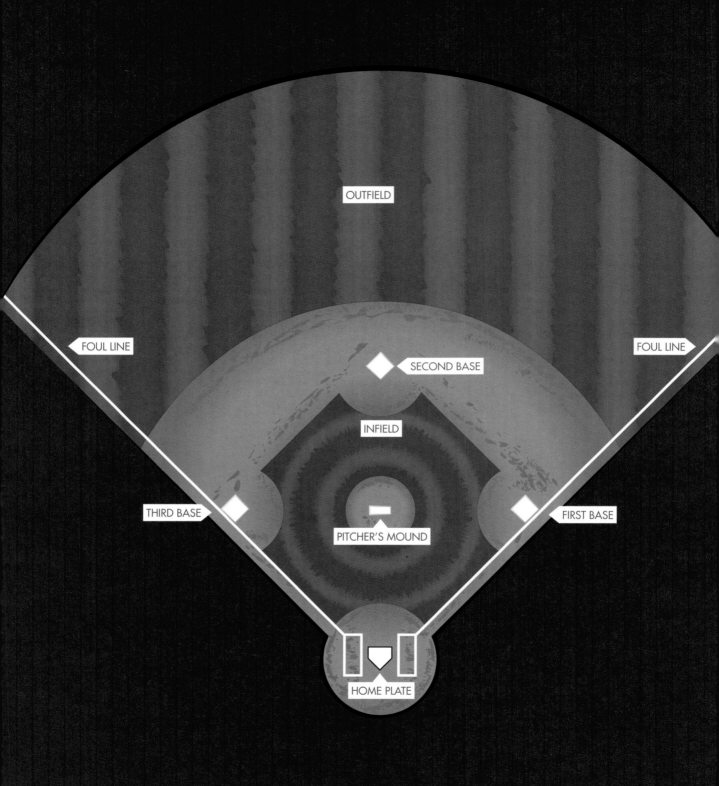

OUTFIELD

FOUL LINE

FOUL LINE

SECOND BASE

INFIELD

THIRD BASE

FIRST BASE

PITCHER'S MOUND

HOME PLATE

The Baseball Diamond

Baseball games are played on a field called a diamond. Four bases form this diamond shape. The bases are 90 feet (27 m) apart. The area around and inside the bases is called the infield. At the center of the infield is the pitcher's mound. The grass area beyond the bases is called the outfield. White lines start at **home plate** and go toward the outfield. These are the foul lines. Baseballs hit outside these lines are out of play unless they are caught by a fielder. The outfield walls are about 300–450 feet (91–137 m) from home plate.

Big Days

The Cubs have had some good seasons in their history. Here are three of them:

1907–08: *A Cubs team led by great pitching won back-to-back World Series championships.*

1984: *Good and bad: The Cubs won the first two games of the NL Championship Series. One more win would send them to the World Series. Then they lost three straight to the San Diego Padres. Once again, the Cubs were disappointed.*

2007–08: *The Cubs made the playoffs two seasons in a row. It was the first time they had done that in 100 years. However, they lost all their games in those two playoff series.*

The Cubs celebrate on the field after winning the 2008 NL Central championship.

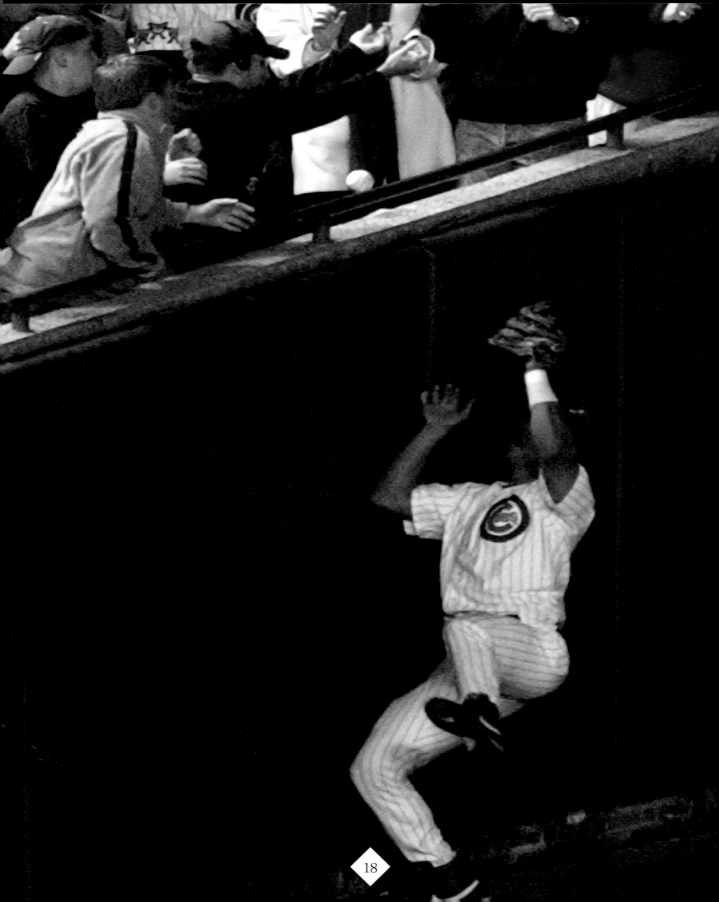

Tough Days

The Cubs have had a lot of tough seasons. Here are three of the worst:

1962: *The Cubs lost 103 games, their worst record ever. They finished next to last in the NL.*

1945: *The Billy Goat Curse bit the Cubbies! A man tried to bring a good-luck goat into a World Series game at Wrigley Field. He and the goat weren't allowed to stay. The man put a "curse" on the team. He said they would never win another World Series. And they haven't.*

2003: *The Cubs were leading 3-0 in the eighth inning. A win would take them to the World Series. But a fan tried to grab a foul ball that would have ended the inning. The Florida Marlins won the game and then knocked the Cubs out of their chance at the Series.*

The fan wearing headphones kept Moises Alou from catching this foul ball in a game against the Florida Marlins.

Meet the Fans

Cubs fans are the most loyal in baseball. They have to be. Their team hasn't won a title in 100 years! They pack Wrigley Field for every game. They started a baseball tradition a few seasons ago. When an opponent hits a home run into the stands, the fans throw it back! Cubs fans also love to watch the games from nearby rooftops.

No matter the weather, Cubs fans always support their team.

Mordecai Brown, Pitcher

Heroes Then . . .

In the 1880s and 1890s, Chicago's Cap Anson was one of the best all-around players. He was the first player to reach 3,000 hits in a career. Mordecai Brown was called "Three-Finger" because he had hurt his hand in a farming accident. He pitched for the Cubs from 1904 to 1912. In 1930, Hack Wilson had 191 runs batted in (RBI). That's still the most ever in one season. In the 1950s and 1960s, Ernie Banks earned the nickname "Mr. Cub." A slugging infielder, he was loved by the fans. One of his favorite sayings was, "It's a beautiful day for a ballgame. . . . Let's play two!" In the 1980s, second baseman Ryne Sandberg was a **Gold Glove** fielder, a top base stealer, and a home run slugger. In the late 1990s and early 2000s, Sammy Sosa had three seasons with 60 or more homers.

Sammy Sosa was a star hitter for the Cubs.

Heroes Now . . .

The Cubs' roster is made up of a group of young stars. Power-hitting first baseman Anthony Rizzo joined the Cubs in 2012. He hit 38 home runs for the Cubs in his first year with the team. Shortstop Starlin Castro led the NL with 207 hits in 2011. Fireballing pitcher Jeff Samardzija gets a lot of strikeouts in each game.

The present-day Cubs are loaded with young stars.

Starlin Castro, Shortstop

Anthony Rizzo, First Base

Jeff Samardzija, Pitcher

BATTING HELMET

TEAM JERSEY

BATTING GLOVES

BAT

TEAM PANTS

26

BASEBALL CLEATS

Gearing Up

Baseball players all wear a team jersey and pants. They have to wear a team hat in the field and a helmet when batting. Take a look at Junior Lake and Dioner Navarro to see some other parts of a baseball player's uniform.

CATCHER'S MASK

CATCHER'S CHEST PROTECTOR

CATCHER'S SHIN GUARD

Dioner Navarro, Catcher

CATCHER'S MITT

On the left: Junior Lake, Outfield

Sports Stats

Here are some all-time career records for the Chicago Cubs. All of the stats are through the 2013 season.

THE BASEBALL

A Major League baseball weighs about 5 ounces (142 g). It is 9 inches (23 cm) around. A leather cover surrounds hundreds of feet of string. That string is wound around a small center of rubber and cork.

HOME RUNS

Sammy Sosa, 545
Ernie Banks, 512

RUNS BATTED IN

Cap Anson, 1,879
Ernie Banks, 1,636

BATTING AVERAGE

Bill Madlock, .336
Riggs Stephenson, .336

STOLEN BASES

Frank Chance, 400
Bill Lange, 399

WINS BY A PITCHER

Charlie Root, 201
Mordecai Brown, 188

WINS BY A MANAGER

Cap Anson, 1,282

EARNED RUN AVERAGE

Mordecai Brown, 1.80
Jack Pfiester, 1.85

Glossary

Gold Glove an award given to the top fielder at each position in each league. In the 1980s, second baseman Ryne Sandberg was a Gold Glove fielder.

home plate a five-sided rubber pad where batters stand to swing. Runners touch home plate to score runs.

loyal supporting something no matter what. Chicago Cubs fans are very loyal to their team.

opponents the teams or players that play against each other. The Cubs' AL opponents change every year.

outfield the large grassy area beyond the infield of a baseball diamond. The outfield fence at Wrigley Field is covered with bright green ivy plants.

rivals teams that play each other often and have an ongoing competition. The Cubs and the Cardinals are rivals.

World Series the Major League Baseball championship. The World Series is played each year between the winners of the American and National Leagues.

Find Out More

BOOKS

Buckley, James Jr. *Eyewitness Baseball*.
New York: DK Publishing, 2010.

Stewart, Mark. *The Chicago Cubs*. Chicago:
Norwood House Press, 2008.

Teitelbaum, Michael. *Baseball*. Ann Arbor,
MI: Cherry Lake Publishing, 2009.

WEB SITES

Visit our Web page for links about the Chicago Cubs and other pro baseball teams: *www.childsworld.com/links*

Note to Parents, Teachers, and Librarians: We routinely verify our Web links to make sure they are safe and active sites. So encourage your readers to check them out!

Index